By Barbara Del Piano

Illustrations By Jackie Black

Published by the Daughters of Hawai'i

He inoa, e Kaleleonālani
Mo'opuna 'oe a Kalai'ōpu'u
Aloha nui 'ia ke Kuini 'Ema
I ka nahenahe mai o kō leo
I ka maika'i o nā 'ōlelo
Piha hau'oli nā maka'āinana
'O ko lākou hoa a'e like ai
Helu 'ekahi o ke aupuni lani
He lani nui 'oe a he hiwahiwa
Hi'ipoi 'ia nei e ka lāhui

This is your name chant, o Kaleleonālani
Descendant of Kalai'ōpu'u
Dearly loved are you, Queen Emma
For the softness of your voice
For the kindness of your words
Thy people are filled with joy
They like to compare you to
The greatest in the kingdom of heaven
You are a great chiefess, dearly beloved
Much praised by your people.

Translation by Theodore Kelsey
He Lei no 'Emalani, Bishop Museum Press 2001

Emma Beloved Queen of Hawaiʻi

The Daughters of Hawaiʻi is deeply grateful to the Queen's Medical Center and the Strong Foundation for funding this publication.

Published in the United States by Daughters of Hawaiʻi
2913 Pali Highway
Honolulu, HI 96817
www.daughtersofhawaii.org

Copyright 2007
Daughters of Hawaiʻi

All rights reserved.

ISBN #0-938851-15-2

Printed in Hong Kong
Design by Bullard & Black Advertising Group Honolulu, HI

First Edition

TABLE OF CONTENTS

Introduction IV
Chapter One – Papa's Little Girl 1
Chapter Two – Emma Goes To School 5
Chapter Three – Dining With The King 11
Chapter Four – A Day At Waikīkī 19
Chapter Five – A Deadly Illness Strikes 23
Chapter Six – Emma's First Grand Ball 27
Chapter Seven – A King Is Proclaimed 33
Chapter Eight – The Proposal 37
Chapter Nine – Wedding Plans 41
Chapter Ten – The Happiest Day 45
Chapter Eleven – A Trip To Kaua'i 51
Chapter Twelve – The Birth Of An Heir 55
Chapter Thirteen – The Queen's Hospital 59
Chapter Fourteen – The Prince Of Hawai'i 65
Chapter Fifteen – The Death Of The King 73
Chapter Sixteen – Emma Visits England 79
Chapter Seventeen – Alaka'i Swamp 85
Chapter Eighteen – Almost A Queen Again 90
Chapter Nineteen – A New Life, Old Memories ... 97
Chapter Twenty – The Queen's Gifts To Her People 103
Emma's Schoolmates 108
Glossary 109

INTRODUCTION

When the famous British explorer, Captain James Cook, arrived at the Hawaiian Islands on January 18, 1778, he found a society ruled by warrior chiefs. Each of the eight main islands was controlled by one or more high chiefs who often went to war against one another for possession of the land. Hawaiʻi, the largest of the islands, was ruled by a high chief named Kalaniopuʻu. One of the warriors in his army was his nephew, Kamehameha. After the death of Kalaniopuʻu, Kamehameha became the ruler of Hawaiʻi. The young chief then set out to conquer all of the other islands. He captured a British seaman named John Young and convinced him to remain in Hawaiʻi to teach his soldiers how to use guns and cannons. When Kamehameha at last succeeded in uniting the islands into one kingdom, Hawaiʻi became a peaceful place. Kamehameha was so grateful to John Young that he gave him a great tract of land, the title of High Chief, and allowed him to marry his niece, a beautiful chiefess named Kaʻoanaʻeha.

As more and more ships from around the world came to Hawaiʻi, the little island kingdom adopted many western customs. Instead of feather capes and helmets, chiefs wore suits and hats. Kamehameha was called King and he ruled justly and wisely, and established laws for the good of all his people. Even though he adopted new customs, he kept many of the old ones.

In old Hawai'i there was a custom, called *hānai*, in which parents gave a newborn child to a close friend or relative as a sign of their deep love and devotion. John Young and his wife had four children; a son named John Young II, and three daughters, Jane, Fanny and Grace.

Thus it happened that when Grace and her English husband, Dr. T. C. B. Rooke, found that they could have no children of their own, Grace's sister Fanny and her husband, Chief Nāe'a, promised them their next child.

The Rookes could hardly wait for the infant to be born, but finally the day came. With other relatives, they gathered at Fanny's home, waiting to welcome the newborn into the world. Then, like a precious belated Christmas gift, a beautiful baby girl was born on January 2, 1836. The infant was wrapped in a piece of soft *kapa* and Grace and Dr. Rooke brought her to their new home. They named their daughter Emma Kalanikaumaka'amano, which means "the chiefess who is looked upon with favor."

At that time, most of the people in Hawai'i lived in grass houses, but Dr. Rooke had built one of the most modern

wooden houses in all of Honolulu, the main seaport and largest town in the Kingdom. Rooke House, as it was called, was a large two-story home with a wide verandah across the front. It sat on a large piece of land, surrounded by tall trees, and fragrant gardens. Dr. Rooke used the main floor of the house for his medical office.

Because Emma's *hānai* father was English and her mother Hawaiian, she grew up as a child of two different cultures. She learned to speak both English and Hawaiian and could easily switch from one language to the other. She felt just as comfortable in a pretty dress with shoes and stockings as she did in a loose *muʻumuʻu*. She loved her beautiful, western-style home, but was just as happy in a grass house. Emma learned to use a knife and fork while eating roasted pheasant, but also enjoyed twirling poi around her finger and eating raw fish with her hands.

Even though her father was a fine doctor and cared for the King and most of the important people in the town, he and Grace worried about Emma, as so many Hawaiian children died in infancy. Although foreigners who visited Hawaiʻi brought many good things, they also brought diseases to which the Hawaiians had never been exposed. Even measles and chicken pox could be deadly because the people had no resistance to them. During the first year of her life, special efforts were made to keep Emma safe and healthy, and even the slightest cold would alarm the household.

When at last Emma's first birthday rolled around, her parents planned a big party for her. It was an old custom in Hawai'i, still practiced today, to have a grand feast to celebrate this event. All of Emma's relatives… her parents, grandparents, aunts, uncles, cousins and friends… came to enjoy the *lu'au*. There was lots of food, including fish, pig, *poi* and fruits of all kinds. Dancers did the hula and chanters praised Emma's beauty, her parents, and her ancestors. In their melodious voices they told of wonderful things to come in Emma's life, and also some very sad things. Most of the people were having too much fun to pay attention to such sad tidings. The few who heard the words wondered if they would come true.

CHAPTER ONE

PAPA'S LITTLE GIRL

Little Emma was a happy baby and soon grew into a delightful child. Her sparkling eyes, fair skin and wavy dark hair proclaimed her mixed heritage and enhanced her beauty. Even though Dr. Rooke was very busy caring for his many patients, he always found time to take little Emma on his knee and talk to her or read a story from one of the books in his large library. Emma's English grandmother often sent packages of books to the Rookes, all the way from London. Many were children's stories that the eager child never tired of hearing. Emma learned to speak proper English at an early age. From her Mama Grace and her *kahu*, Malama, she learned to speak Hawaiian.

Papa taught Emma to read when she was very young and she learned quickly. Soon she was reading the books her English grandmother sent, barely stumbling over the words.

Although her own life was filled with happiness, Emma soon learned that there were many people who were not as fortunate as she. Each morning, just after waking, Emma would glance out of her window to see Papa's patients forming a long line to the door of his dispensary. It made her sad to see so many mothers carrying sick children, older people hobbling on homemade canes, and others who had slings or splints on broken limbs. After seeing patients in his own dispensary, Dr. Rooke ordered his horse and buggy and visited those who were too ill to leave their homes. Many patients were poor and could not afford to pay Papa, but he never asked them for money. To show their appreciation, the patients often brought fish or a hand-carved wooden bowl filled with fresh *poi*. Sometimes they would bring a *lauhala* basket full of bananas, *kalo* or sweet potatoes they had grown.

Early in life Emma saw pain and misery and would always have deep compassion for those who suffered.

Sometimes when he could get away for a while, Papa took Emma driving in the horse-drawn buggy up to Nuʻuanu

Valley where it was cool and green. Dr. Rooke had a large farm there where he grew coffee and sugar cane. Emma loved the stories Papa told her as the buggy rolled along the bumpy road. She enjoyed hearing about his home in England, and the young Queen Victoria who became queen of the British Empire when she was just eighteen years old. Dr. Rooke had already left England before the beginning of Victoria's long reign, but he had heard and read many things about her and Emma eagerly listened to his tales. Her young mind devoured his descriptions of life at the royal court in London.

Emma never dreamed that she too would one day be a queen and that she would visit England as a guest of the great Queen Victoria. But many things would happen in Emma's life before those events took place.

CHAPTER TWO

EMMA GOES TO SCHOOL

Emma had just turned six years of age when a message was delivered to Rooke House. It was an invitation to Emma to attend the Chiefs' Children's School. This was a very special school established by the King, Kamehameha III, for the children of the highest chiefs in the Kingdom. It was a great honor to attend the school and Dr. and Mrs. Rooke were very pleased that Emma had been chosen. They were also sad because Emma had never been away from home before and they knew that they would miss her.

That evening, when Mama and Papa told Emma that she would be going to school, and that she would be living

there, the frightened child ran crying to her room. Mama and Papa spent many hours trying to convince Emma how wonderful it would be to go to school. They told her that she would make many new friends and learn all sorts of wonderful things, but Emma was not convinced.

When the first day of school arrived, Dr. Rooke ordered the carriage very early and Grace tiptoed into Emma's room before daybreak to gently waken the sleeping child. Hardly a word was spoken as the family sat down to breakfast. Emma could barely swallow a mouthful of the luscious fruit in the bowl before her. Even the freshly baked bread, still warm from the oven, didn't appeal to her.

Finally it was time to go. Dr. Rooke gently took Emma's hand, and together they walked outside and climbed into the buggy while Mama waved from the *lānai* as the buggy rumbled down the long driveway.

A high stone wall surrounded the school and Emma thought that it looked very much like a prison. The couple who stood waiting at the gate seemed very tall and stern. Tightly clutching Papa's hand, Emma tried to hide behind him. Then, quite in a daze, she allowed Mrs. Cooke to take her other hand and lead her across the yard and into the building, tears blurring her vision so that she could barely see.

Once inside, the other students gathered around as Mrs. Cooke introduced Emma to her classmates. The only one she knew was her cousin, Peter Kaeo. She learned that the tall, handsome boy named Alexander was a prince and heir to Kamehameha III. Since the King had no children of his own, he had adopted his nephew, Alexander Liholiho, who was also known as 'Iolani. Then there were Alexander's brothers, Moses and Lot, and his sister, Victoria. Two other brothers, James and David, stood quietly by while their younger sister, Lydia, who was barely four years old, giggled as she stared curiously at the newcomer. Two sisters named Jane and Abigail were introduced, along with a slender serious boy named William. Finally, there were three girls named Polly, Bernice and Elizabeth. All of the names and faces seemed to melt together and Emma was bewildered as she looked from one to the other through her tears.

It was a relief to see Peter smiling at her. Then she realized that the others were smiling too, and suddenly it didn't seem quite so terrible.

Introductions over, the students returned to their school work and Emma found that she was able to read,

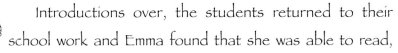

write and spell nearly as well as most of the other students. When music class began, Bernice, who was a few years older, took her place at the piano and played while the others sang. Emma loved music, and before long she found herself singing along with them.

    The day passed quickly, and when it was time for bed, Emma followed Mrs. Cooke into a small room with a high window. Elizabeth, who was to be her roommate, was already there, busily turning down the *kapa* coverlet on her bed. Emma had never had to do anything for herself but she quietly watched Elizabeth and turned down her own coverlet and climbed into bed.

 Emma was frightened and lonely. How she missed Mama and Papa! She longed for her big koa bed with its high posts and soft pillows. How she missed the big window with the dainty lace curtains from which she could look down on the trees and gardens at Rooke House! How she wished that Malama was there to help her undress and turn down her bed just as she did at home. The night seemed very long and lonely as Emma lay there, tears quietly rolling down her cheeks, until she finally fell asleep.

CHAPTER THREE

DINING WITH THE KING

When Emma opened her eyes the next morning and glanced at the unfamiliar scene about her, she wanted to cry all over again. Instead, she fought back her tears and looked around the small room. Elizabeth was already up and dressed. As Emma slowly climbed out of the narrow, hard bed, Elizabeth explained that the students were expected to make their beds just as soon as they were out of them. Since Emma had never made a bed before, Elizabeth showed her how to fluff the pillow and pull the covers tight and tuck them in. Then together they straightened the *kapa* coverlet so that all the sides were even.

Emma found the routine of school life difficult at first. Each morning the children assembled in the parlor. Then, with Mr. Cooke in the lead, they would set off on a long walk before breakfast. On the very first day, Emma tore the sleeve of her dress as she brushed against a thorny bush along the narrow path. Later, she asked Mrs. Cooke to send for Malama to bring her a new dress. Mrs. Cooke frowned and explained that the sleeve could easily be mended.

"Then," said Emma, "May I please send for Malama to mend it?" Shaking her head, Mrs. Cooke led Emma to a big chest. She opened a drawer and brought out a large wooden box which Emma soon learned was the sewing box. Mrs. Cooke sat Emma down on a bench and showed her how to thread the needle and weave it in and out of the cloth. Emma was quite annoyed at having to perform such a lowly task, but when Mrs. Cooke praised her tiny stitches and the good job she was doing, Emma didn't feel quite so bad. In fact, when she had finished, she could hardly see where the tear had been.

Although Emma missed Mama and Papa, the days were so busy that she soon found little time to be homesick. Emma never imagined that there would be so many things to learn. Besides reading, writing and arithmetic, the students learned geography, history, and composition. The boys were taught chemistry and geometry while the girls learned to sew, embroider, and cook. Emma's favorite class was music. Bernice helped Mrs. Cooke teach Emma and Lydia to play the piano. All the children had fine singing voices and were often asked to perform when parents or other visitors came to the school. The children also spent a good part of each day praying and reading the Bible. On Sundays, they wore their best clothes and marched two by two from the school to the white coral church down the road to attend services.

One day Mrs. Cooke announced that the King, Kamehameha III, and many of the chiefs were coming to visit. School was dismissed early so the eager children could help the Cookes get ready for the big event. The King's servants delivered huge baskets of fish, *kalo*, sweet potatoes, coconuts, a whole barrel of *poi* and other delicious food that would be prepared for the King's dinner. Because he was known to be especially fond of cake, Mrs. Cooke spent the day baking cakes. She made so many that when she was finished, she found that she had used nearly four dozen eggs and all the flour and sugar in the pantry.

When the King and chiefs arrived, there was a grand feast. Everyone ate so much that there was almost no room for dessert, but when the cakes were brought out, they looked so delicious that everyone had a piece… and then another… and another.

After dinner the students showed the King samples of their schoolwork and recited passages from the Bible. Then the children gathered around the piano and sang as Bernice and Emma, and even little Lydia, took turns playing. When the evening finally came to an end and the children went to bed, Emma was so excited she could hardly sleep.

CHAPTER FOUR

A DAY AT WAIKĪKĪ

The students worked hard at school and, if they had been very good and did well in their studies, Mr. Cooke sometimes planned a special outing. One day he arranged for the students to ride their horses to Waikīkī, a distance of nearly four miles. Each student carried a bundle of food for a picnic lunch.

The sky was clear and sparkling blue when the students set out early in the morning. The horses' hooves clomped along the bumpy road, sending clouds of dust swirling into the air. They sang and laughed and waved at the people they passed along the way, and of course, the people waved back.

After riding for more than an hour, thousands of coconut palms came into view along the shore, with small villages of grass houses nestled under the towering fronds. Toward the mountains, they passed acres of fish ponds, where fat mullet swam beneath the murky water fed by mountain streams. *Kalo* patches, with thousands of heart-shaped leaves of brilliant green, glistened in the sunlight. Instead of brown dirt, the ground beneath them was now white and sandy and the horses' hooves sank into it.

As they neared the shore at Waikīkī, a grass house,

larger than the others, appeared. This was the King's beach house, and although the King himself was away, the children were invited to visit. Another grass house nearby was filled with long, wooden surfboards and Alexander and David raced ahead of the others, eager to paddle out and ride the waves back to shore. James, Lot, Moses, Peter and William galloped close behind. Quickly tethering their horses to a post, they rushed to take a board and plunge into the water, paddling out to the breaking waves. The boys vied with each other to see who could stand upright on the board for the longest time. Alexander usually won.

The older girls, Jane, Bernice, and Abigail, sat on the shore, watching over the younger children. Elizabeth, Emma, and Polly gleefully splashed each other, laughing as they ran in and out of the sparkling aquamarine water.

Later the girls walked along the beach picking up colorful seashells and pieces of coral from the water's edge. Mr. Cooke and the boys went fishing, throwing huge nets into the water as schools of *pāpi'o, akule* and *moi* swam by. When they pulled up the nets, they were filled with plump, glistening fish. The boys gathered branches and leaves that had fallen on the ground and tossed them into a big pile. Mr. Cooke started a fire and they cleaned and cooked the fish they had caught. Hungry after so much activity, the students quickly devoured the delicious meal. They husked young, green coconuts and quenched their thirst with the cool liquid inside the shells.

After they had had their fill, everyone sat around the fire and sang. The sound of their clear, young voices wafted down the beach and soon the villagers came out of their houses and gathered along the shore to listen.

The sun was low in the sky when Mr. Cooke announced that it was time to go. It had been such a lovely day that nobody wanted to leave. Tired but happy, they gathered their belongings, mounted their horses, and began the long ride back to school. Later that night, lying in their beds, Emma and Elizabeth whispered late into the night about the fun they had. They both agreed it had been one of the happiest days of their life at school.

CHAPTER FIVE

A DEADLY ILLNESS STRIKES

Emma had been attending school for nearly six years when a deadly epidemic raged through Honolulu late in 1848. Honolulu was a busy seaport; every day its harbor was filled with ships from many parts of the world. They came from such places as England, France, Russia, the United States and Japan. They carried cargo of all kinds, including tools, furniture, clothing, and mail. One ship carried something else... the deadly measles virus. The illness quickly spread among the Hawaiian people, and in a short time, hundreds had come down with the sickness.

All of the students at the Chiefs' Children's School were taken ill. Dr. Rooke and the other doctors in the Kingdom worked day and night to treat the victims as best they could, and to try to stop the spread of the deadly disease. Mr. Cooke helped the doctors make medicines for the sick and joined them as they went about town trying to ease the suffering. Meanwhile, Mrs. Cooke tended the sick students and her own children as well.

Emma, who had been only mildly ill, recovered quickly. She joined Dr. Rooke, traveling from one end of town to the other, stopping to give food and medicine to the sick. So many people were stricken that it was impossible to reach them all, although they started out in the early morning and continued late into the night.

When the epidemic was finally over, hundreds of people were dead, including chiefs and commoners. One of the first victims was Moses, the older brother of Lot, Alexander and Victoria. James, the older brother of David and Lydia, and their little sister Kaʻiminaʻuao, who was about to enter school, were also stricken and could not be saved. It was a sad time for the people of Honolulu. Nearly every family lost a loved one. Emma thought a lot about the need for a hospital. She wondered how many lives might have been saved if there had been one.

Not long after the town had recovered from the tragedy, the school, now called the Royal School, closed. Many of the older children had left and Mr. and Mrs. Cooke were exhausted from so many years of hard work. The students went home to their own families. Some of them, like Lydia and Elizabeth, attended a day school. Others, including Emma, had private tutors.

Miss Sarah Von Phister, an English governess, who was engaged to teach Emma, came to live in the Rooke household where she and Emma soon became fast friends. Each morning, Miss Von Phister and Emma met in the upstairs parlor. The tutor taught her pupil to speak French and nourished her love of literature as they spent many hours reading poetry and French and English classics. In the afternoon, Emma helped Papa in the dispensary. Her new life suited her well.

    Although Emma enjoyed her years at school, she was happy to be home once again. She was no longer a little girl, but a lovely, gifted and well-educated young woman.

CHAPTER SIX

EMMA'S FIRST GRAND BALL

Emma and her former schoolmates saw each other often. Horseback riding was a favorite pastime and Emma and Alexander, along with David, Elizabeth, William and the others, frequently rode their horses into Nuʻuanu Valley. There they swam in a pool of clear, sparkling water, surrounded by fragrant wild ginger blossoms. They picked the delicate blooms and fashioned them into *lei* to wear on their heads or around their necks. Emma liked to venture far back into the valley and she and Alexander often rode together, side by side. At the end of the narrow dirt road, the land dropped off suddenly and a sheer cliff went straight down hundreds of feet. It was an awesome sight because from this high place on the rugged Koʻolau mountains one could gaze at the bright blue ocean on the other side of the island. Sometimes Emma and Alexander rode down the narrow winding path to a tiny village called Kailua. Emma was impressed with Alexander's gentlemanly manners as he helped her up when she mounted her horse, or took her hand to help her down at the end of the ride.

All of the young people loved to dance and often got together to learn the very latest steps. There were parties,

sometimes at Bernice's house, sometimes at Emma's, where they practiced the schottische from Scotland, the lancers from England, the polka from Czechoslovakia or the Virginia reel from America. It took hours of practice because they all danced together in one big square or circle and everyone had to keep in step with the others.

One day a messenger from the King came to Rooke House and delivered an invitation. Not only were Dr. and Mrs. Rooke invited to attend a ball in honor of Queen Kalama's birthday at 'Iolani Palace, but Emma was invited as well.

Mama had several pretty gowns, but since this would be Emma's first formal affair, she had nothing quite grand enough to wear. Fortunately, Emma had learned to sew very well, so she decided to make her first ball gown, and Mama and Miss Von Phister offered to help. The three of them went to town one afternoon to look for just the right fabric. They examined bolt after bolt of lovely silks and laces and finally chose a pale blue satin they all decided was the perfect color. They worked on the dress, hand-sewing it with tiny stitches and adorning it with lustrous seed pearls around the neck and bodice. The finished garment looked so fashionable it might have been ordered from Paris or New York.

When the night of the ball arrived, Papa had the carriage brought to the front door of Rooke House. He helped Mama and Emma up the high steps and saw that they were comfortably settled in the leather seats before climbing up to join them. As they approached the Palace, the sparkling lights of the gas chandeliers glowed in the darkness. The Royal Hawaiian Band was playing, and flowers and ferns were set about in tall vases throughout the spacious rooms. The guests looked elegant; the ladies in lovely gowns, most of the men in full dress uniform. In the ballroom, each guest was presented to the King and Queen, with Alexander, as heir to the throne, standing beside them. Emma thought that he looked ever so handsome.

When the dancing started, Alexander was at her side. Taking her arm in his, he led Emma to the dance floor. The tall, handsome Prince in his crisp military uniform and the petite, graceful young lady made a striking couple as they glided across the floor, flawlessly performing the intricate steps they had practiced so many times.

The night ended far too soon and suddenly the ball was over and it was time to say goodbye. Alexander took Emma aside and told her that he and his brother Lot would soon be leaving on a long trip. They would visit America and

England, and probably France, with Dr. Gerrit P. Judd, the nation's Minister of Finance, as chaperon. The trip would take several months. Emma pretended to be happy, but she felt sad to think that Alexander would be leaving. When they said goodbye, he took her hand in his and smiled. "I'll miss you," he whispered, and Emma nodded. She knew that she would miss him too.

CHAPTER SEVEN

A KING IS PROCLAIMED

To Emma, it seemed forever since Alexander had sailed away with Lot and Dr. Judd. Newspaper reports described the travels of the young Princes, and Emma eagerly devoured accounts of their journey across the United States. One article told of their hunting wild turkeys in Michigan; another, their trip to Illinois so that Dr. Judd could visit his mother. Emma laughed when she read about a brief stop in Halifax, Nova Scotia, on the way to England. Alexander and Lot went on a sleigh ride shortly before the ship departed, and nearly missed the boat.

There was no news for several weeks while the ship crossed the Atlantic and Emma impatiently waited to hear about their arrival. Articles resumed when the ship reached Liverpool and the Hawaiian delegation proceeded to

London. Emma could barely imagine the exciting lives they were living. The stories told about important diplomatic functions and parties and visits to famous cathedrals and museums. When they attended the theater in London to see a Shakespearean play, they were seated in the Queen's box. The Princes toured Buckingham Palace as guests of Prince Albert, Queen Victoria's husband.

After their sojourn in England, Alexander and Lot traveled to France. Emma read that while in Paris the young men enjoyed the opera and even managed to take a few fencing lessons. Wherever they went, they were treated with all the honor and respect afforded visiting royalty.

Emma felt her life at home very dull in comparison, and even the company of friends failed to cheer her up. When a handsome young British naval officer invited her to elegant parties aboard his ship, horseback rides, and moonlight carriage rides, Emma found excuses to decline.

It had been nearly a year since their departure when word finally arrived that Alexander and Lot were coming home. Hundreds of people flocked to the waterfront to see the ship as it sailed into Honolulu Harbor. Emma was barely able to catch a glimpse of the young men as they strode down the gangplank, smiling broadly and waving at the crowd. They looked taller and older than she remembered. Alexander, she thought, was more handsome than ever.

Not long after their return, King Kamehameha III held a reception at 'Iolani Palace to welcome the travelers. As Emma stood with her parents in the long line, she watched Alexander shaking hands and laughing with friends and acquaintances. When finally she stood face to face with him, she blushed as he complimented her on her elegant gown and remarked on what a beautiful young lady she had become.

Now that Alexander was home, Emma eagerly looked forward to the parties and outings the young people planned. Although Alexander attended many of them, Emma noticed that he looked tired and worried much of the time. She knew it was because he was involved in making important decisions with the King. She also knew that there were problems with foreign countries like France and England. Then the King became ill and the burden of governing fell even more heavily on the shoulders of the young Prince. The King's condition worsened until finally he died after a reign of nearly thirty years. Alexander was just twenty years old when, as heir to the throne, he was proclaimed monarch of the Hawaiian

Kingdom and given the name Kamehameha IV.

Sitting with her parents in the audience as Alexander gave his inaugural speech, Emma listened carefully to every word he uttered. When she heard him say: "Today we begin a new era. Let it be one of… progress, industry, temperance, morality and all those virtues which mark a nation's progress," Emma knew that Alexander would be a wise and honorable ruler.

CHAPTER EIGHT

THE PROPOSAL

Emma had not seen Alexander for several weeks. She knew how busy he was with affairs of state but she missed him very much. It was hard to imagine that Alexander was actually the King of Hawai'i and that he was now addressed as "Your Majesty." She understood that he was making important decisions that affected the country. No wonder he had little time for parties and picnics! Emma kept busy reading, sewing and helping Papa in the dispensary. There were always so many sick people. If only there was a hospital where they could go to be cared for!

One day Emma attended a *lū'au* at Waikīkī. It was a beautiful sunny day and guests were enjoying music and hula. Just as the food was removed from the *imu*, all activi-

ty came to a halt and all eyes turned toward the entrance. The King had arrived, accompanied by a group of officers. After greeting the guests, he strode over to Emma who was seated on a *lauhala* mat, chatting with her friends. He sat down beside her and soon they were engrossed in conversation. The rest of the afternoon flew by as Emma and Alexander laughed and talked and ate the delicious food. When it was time to leave, Alexander insisted on accompanying Emma home. They mounted their horses, and with their friends, started back toward town, the sweet sound of music and the fragrant scent of *pikake* and ginger lingering in the air.

 Emma wished the ride would never end. They slowed their horses so that soon they found themselves well behind the others, riding alone along the quiet road. Twilight descended and the sky was swathed in a brilliant glow as though a brush, dipped in orange paint, had streaked across the heavens. As they approached the spring at Kamōʻiliʻili, they reined in their horses and dismounted, admiring the beauty around them. They stood quietly beneath a stand of tall coconut trees that waved their fronds gently in the trade winds wafting down from Mānoa Valley. The silence was broken when Alexander reached for her hand and, holding it tightly in both of his, asked Emma to be his wife. Emma could scarcely breathe as she listened to Alexander profess his love. When she tried to reply, no words would come. For several seconds she gazed at the tall, handsome man before her. Then she smiled and nodded her head.

Emma barely remembered the ride home. The sky had darkened and stars twinkled overhead. It was truly a magical evening.

When the happy couple reached Rooke House, Dr. and Mrs. Rooke were sitting on the *lānai* enjoying the cool evening breeze. They could tell by the look on Emma's and Alexander's faces, and the joyful manner in which they leapt from their horses, that something exciting had happened. When they heard the news, Mama threw her arms around Emma and hugged her close while Papa vigorously clasped Alexander's hand, pumping it up and down. Later, he wondered if it was an impolite way to treat a king. It was then he realized that his darling Emma was going to be a queen.

CHAPTER NINE

WEDDING PLANS

Word of the engagement spread quickly and there was great rejoicing throughout the Kingdom. The people were happy that there would soon be a beautiful Queen to stand beside their handsome King.

Not everyone took the news well, however. Some of the chiefs complained that Emma was not of high enough rank to marry the King. One jealous chief visited Alexander and told the King that his own daughter was of higher birth than Emma and that he should marry her instead. Alex firmly rejected the suggestion. His heart and mind were made up and there would be no one but Emma! However, the Privy Council had something to say in the matter, as the law required that they approve the match.

When Emma heard of the grumbling of some of the chiefs, she was deeply saddened and ran crying to her room, her happiness momentarily shattered. She waited impatiently for the day when the Privy Council would hand down its decision. That morning, worried friends and relatives gathered at Rooke House to await the announcement. After several hours of suspenseful waiting, a messenger arrived. The Council had overwhelmingly expressed its approval and proclaimed that

the marriage would take place. Everyone breathed a sigh of relief and began to plan the wedding.

A beautiful gown of white silk with a long train and embroidered flounces was ordered from a fashion house in New York. Several months later a ship from England arrived and a large box was unloaded and delivered to Rooke House. It contained a special gift from Queen Victoria to the young bride-to-be. With trembling hands Emma opened the box and there, nestled in reams of soft tissue, was a beautiful, long veil of exquisite Brussels lace. "Imagine," she cried, "the Queen of England has sent this lovely gift to me. I shall surely be properly dressed for my wedding."

The days flew by. There were dancing parties at night and tea parties in the afternoon. There were so many arrangements to be made and details to be taken care of that Mama and Emma were busy every moment, with barely time enough to think or eat. Then, at last, the long awaited day approached.

It was late when Emma finally went upstairs to bed but she was much too excited to sleep. Clutching her *kihei pili*, she climbed down from the feather bed and crossed the room to gaze out the window. Gentle trade winds caused the sheer curtains to flutter in the moonlight on this balmy May night.

Emma's heart pounded as she thought about tomorrow. It would be the most important day of her life, the day she had been planning and dreaming about for nearly a year. Tomorrow she would become not only the wife of Alexander Liholiho, but Queen of the Hawaiian Islands.

Despite her joy, Emma felt sad at the thought of leaving her parents and the home she loved so well. Then she remembered Papa taking her in his arms and telling her that she would always be his little girl and that he and Mama would always be there for her.

Emma prayed that she would be strong enough to fulfill the duties of her new role. She knew Alexander was under a great deal of pressure from foreign countries that vied with each other to extract special privileges from the small nation. She knew Alexander had the strength of character to stand up for his country and prayed that she would be a proper helpmate for him and that together they would accomplish many good things for the Hawaiian people.

It was nearly dawn when Emma finally fell asleep. In the morning, when Mama Grace tiptoed into the room, she found her daughter curled up in the *koa* rocking chair beside the open window. A tear rolled down her cheek as she gazed lovingly at Emma. She prayed that she and Alexander would have a long and happy life together. But first, they must worry about getting through the day.

CHAPTER TEN

THE HAPPIEST DAY

Emma glanced nervously at the tall grandfather clock in the hallway. The morning had flown by and it was nearly time for the carriage to arrive that would take them the few blocks to the beautiful white coral church where the wedding would take place. It was May 18, 1856, and Emma Rooke, twenty years old, was soon to become the wife of Alexander Liholiho and Queen of the Hawaiian Kingdom.

The sky was a brilliant blue; not long before, a light rain, considered a blessing by the Hawaiians, had swept down from Nu'uanu Valley and quickly blown out to sea. Again the sky was cloudless, befitting the historic event that was soon to take place. This would be the first royal Christian wedding in the history of Hawai'i.

The excitement heightened as Emma's bridesmaids

began to arrive. Her cousin Mary Pittman, Lydia Paki, and Alexander's sister, Victoria, all looked lovely in their beautiful satin gowns of pale yellow. So did her maid of honor, Lucy Peabody, and bridesmaid Elizabeth Kekaʻaniau Pratt, her dear friend since they were roommates at the Chiefs' Children's School. But Emma outshone them all! Her white silk wedding dress and the exquisite veil were perfection itself on her slender body. Orange blossoms and roses, woven into a crown, complemented her natural crown of silky black hair. Around her throat she proudly wore a glittering diamond necklace, a gift from Alexander.

Emma barely remembered the carriage ride. She was hardly aware of the thousands of people who lined the streets, waving and shouting their best wishes. Businesses and stores were closed, for the day had been proclaimed a holiday. All of Honolulu turned out to catch a glimpse of the beautiful bride as she smiled from the window of the carriage. The handsome groom, with his brother Lot and father, Governor Kekūanaōʻa, traveled the same route in another carriage. A cavalry escort of uniformed soldiers led the procession and another brought up the rear. Horsemen carrying feather *kāhili* flanked both carriages.

    As they approached the church, Emma was barely aware of the sounds of the Royal Hawaiian Band. Five hundred guests filled every seat in Kawaiahaʻo Church and others stood in the doorways to witness the ceremony. Thousands more milled about the church grounds. Emma's heart pounded as she walked down the long aisle of the church on Papa's arm, preceded by her lovely bridesmaids.

    Then suddenly, there was Alexander standing beside her. He looked so handsome in his blue uniform trimmed with gold embroidery. Gold epaulettes made his broad shoulders look even broader.

    The Reverend Richard Armstrong began the service which proceeded flawlessly until Alexander's brother, Lot, who was best man, discovered that he had forgotten the wedding ring. After a few minutes of confusion, he borrowed a ring from a member of the wedding party and handed it to his brother. Although it was much too big, Alexander placed the gold band on Emma's delicate finger and soon the ceremony was over.

    With cannons booming from the hillside above, and crowds cheering wildly, the wedding party returned to the Palace where members of the diplomatic and consular corps were waiting to greet them. With glasses of champagne held high, representatives of many foreign countries around the world toasted the newlyweds with wishes for a long and happy life.

The line of guests stretched from the Throne Room of 'Iolani Palace, out the door and down the long hallway to the entrance. Although Emma was beginning to tire, she kept a bright smile on her face as she accepted good wishes from hundreds of people who had come to pay their respects to the King and his new Queen. As the guests arrived, the royal chamberlain announced their names in a loud voice. Many Hawaiians practiced the ancient custom of lying down on the floor and crawling to the royal personages. The European gentlemen bowed deeply, while the ladies curtsied. Some Americans did likewise, while others simply offered a hand. Emma wasn't used to being called "Your Majesty," or being treated in such a regal manner. As a chiefess, she had always received special attention, but as Queen, it was almost more than she could bear. She longed for the quiet, informal life at Rooke House but she knew that she must accept this new way of life as part of her marriage to Alexander and her duty as Queen.

CHAPTER ELEVEN

A TRIP TO KAUA'I

In the excitement of the past year, Emma had given little thought to what life in the palace would be like. Now she was finding that nearly every evening was filled with official functions. There were balls and dancing parties, formal dinners, *lū'au* and teas. It seemed that she was always surrounded by people, most of whom she barely knew. During the day, the palace was filled with government officials, foreign diplomats, or businessmen who came to meet with the King. In the evenings they were frequently occupied with social functions. It was only after returning to their private home on the palace grounds that they could be alone.

It was customary in Hawai'i for a new king to make a grand tour of his realm in order to greet his subjects. In keeping with this tradition, Emma and Alexander traveled completely around the island of O'ahu. Alexander announced one day that it was now time to travel to the neighboring islands. Although these trips would be part of her official duties, Emma was delighted at the thought of getting away from the formal life at court. The preparations for the voyage took several weeks as a ship was specially remodeled to accommodate the King and Queen and their large party. When it was finally time to sail, Emma was amazed to find that nearly two hundred people would be accompanying them, including relatives, friends, other *ali'i*, members of the King's staff, servants and their families.

They first journeyed to the lovely island of Kaua'i, where frequent rains kept the land lush and green. They traveled on horseback, sometimes for hours at a time. Emma loved to ride and never tired of the strenuous exercise. Wherever they went, from village to village, the royal party was welcomed with great joy and feasts were prepared and entertainment provided. It was a very special occasion to be honored by the presence of the King and Queen and the people were eager to pay homage to their rulers.

After spending several days in the little town of Waimea, Emma, Alexander, and their large party set out early one morning to continue their journey. Along the way, they found themselves not far from a place called Nohili, where high sand dunes, some a hundred feet tall, stretched out along the shore. Today, the area is more frequently called Barking Sands because the clapping of hands or shuffling of feet in the sand sounds just like the noise of barking dogs.

Emma and Alexander led the procession down the path to the beach where everyone plunged into the cool water and ran up and down the dunes, clapping and stomping and laughing at the sounds their motions made. Emma scampered up one of the highest dunes with her uncle, Keoni Ana, and Alexander's sister, Victoria. Feeling silly after all the weeks of behaving so properly, they all lay down on the top of the sandy hill, and taking hold of each other's feet, slid down the steep slope. It sounded as though they were being chased by a pack of wild dogs.

That evening they boarded the ship that would take them back to Honolulu. Soon they would continue the pilgrimage with trips to the islands of Hawai'i, Maui, Moloka'i, Lana'i, Kaho'olawe and Ni'ihau. Perhaps because it was their first trip together, Emma would always remember their time on Kaua'i, and the friendly people and relaxing times she and Alexander enjoyed there. The afternoon at Nohili would remain a special memory because there, for just a little while, she could laugh and play and forget that she was a queen.

CHAPTER TWELVE

THE BIRTH OF AN HEIR

Although Emma had been feeling tired for some time, she supposed that her lack of energy was due to the busy schedule she kept. Dr. Rooke was concerned and insisted she have a medical checkup. The results confirmed that Emma was going to have a baby. She was thrilled and Alexander was very proud and happy.

Emma and Alexander wanted to keep the news secret for awhile, but the word soon spread and throughout the Kingdom there was great rejoicing. The months passed quickly as Emma continued to keep her appointments and attend dinners and state functions. As the time drew near, excitement in the royal household grew by leaps and bounds. From the lowliest servant to the King himself, the waiting became more and more difficult.

Finally, on May 20, 1858, Emma knew the time had come and Dr. Rooke and his colleague, Dr. William Hillebrand, were summoned. Alexander hovered nervously at the side of the bed, clasping Emma's small hand in his larger one. In the adjoining room the anxious family waited; both Emma's *hānai* mother, Grace, and her birth mother, Fanny, were there; Alexander's father, Governor Kekūanaō'a, and his brother Lot nervously paced up and down the hall. Aunts and cousins as well as Alexander's sister, Victoria, sat silently, praying that all would go well. Outside on the lawn, dozens of friends, retainers and townspeople gathered to join the vigil. The streets were lined with people eagerly awaiting the royal birth.

It was late in the afternoon when the child, a beautiful healthy son, was born. The town went wild with excitement as the great event was announced by the firing of cannon from the slopes of Punchbowl, the huge crater just above the town. The booms echoed throughout Honolulu and the sound of cheers and laughter rang from the mountains to the sea. From the palace to the harbor, and up to the valleys, the celebrating began and continued through the night. An heir to the throne was born! The noble Kamehameha dynasty would live on!

The celebrations continued throughout the next day when a holiday was declared and all shops and businesses were closed. Flags and bunting fluttered in the breeze as great crowds of people wandered up and down the streets, offering a toast to the baby. The Privy Council met to designate the new-born heir to the throne as "Ka Haku o Hawai'i," the

Prince of Hawai'i. The full name given to the child was Albert Edward Kauikeaouli Leiopapa ā Kamehameha, a long name indeed for such a little one. The name Albert was chosen in honor of Prince Albert, Queen Victoria's husband.

Word spread as ships carried the news throughout the Kingdom, and to America and Europe beyond. Many of the King's subjects traveled to O'ahu from their homes on other islands, bearing gifts for the little Prince. From one end of the Kingdom to the other, they proposed toasts, held *lū'au* or attended church services to celebrate the happy event. Never had the little island Kingdom seen such spontaneous joy at the birth of a child.

A magnificent cradle of beautifully grained *koa*, *kou* and *kamani* woods, exquisitely carved, was made for the baby by the finest cabinetmaker in all of Honolulu. Emma loved to sit beside it and watch "Baby" as he slept, her fingers gently swaying the cradle back and forth. She marveled at his tiny hands and feet and the silkiness of his wavy black hair. Alexander often joined her and together they would silently gaze at the sleeping infant. Every move that the precious baby made and every sound that passed from his tiny lips was like music to their ears. As Emma and Alexander gazed at their beloved infant, they imagined the time when their son would be grown into a fine and honorable man who would carry on the proud Kamehameha heritage. Their happiness was now complete.

CHAPTER THIRTEEN

THE QUEEN'S HOSPITAL

Ever since Emma was old enough to help Papa in his dispensary, she dreamed of a hospital for the sick people of the Kingdom. Now she felt that the time had come to do something about it. Alexander had already asked the legislature for money to build a hospital but nothing had been done. Now the King and Queen decided to take the matter into their own hands.

One morning the King rose early, and after a quick breakfast, kissed Emma and little Kauikeaouli and set off on foot to the business section of town. Dressed in a white linen suit and straw hat, Alexander, with a notebook under his arm, was accompanied by his secretary, Henry Neilson.

Their first stop was at the office of Mr. Hopkins. As they entered, the gentleman was busily looking over his ledger. When he looked up and recognized the King, Mr. Hopkins leaped from his desk to greet the important visitors, wondering what could possibly have brought the King himself to his humble establishment. After exchanging pleasantries, Alexander lost no time relating the reason for his visit. He was there, he explained, to ask Mr. Hopkins and all the chiefs and businessmen of the town to donate money to build a hospital. He told Mr. Hopkins how important it was to the Kingdom to be able to take care of the sick and how sad it was that Honolulu did not have a hospital for the native Hawaiian people. Of course Mr. Hopkins was only too happy to pledge money to the Hospital Fund. How could anyone possibly refuse the King? Alexander smiled as he carefully wrote Mr. Hopkins' name in his notebook. Next to it, he entered a generous figure.

All day long, Alexander and Henry walked about the town, knocking on doors of homes and entering shops and offices. They called on chiefs, residents, shopkeepers and business people. Even the officials in the King's own government were asked to contribute to the Hospital Fund. They were all surprised to see the King and after hearing the reason for his visit, eagerly added their names to the growing list of donors in the King's notebook. Late that afternoon, returning to the Palace, a tired Alexander and Henry, joined by the Queen, sat down and added up the figures. They were amazed at how much money had been promised.

For the next week, Alexander and Henry set off for town each morning, the King carrying his notebook prominently under his arm. Each afternoon when they returned, Emma would be waiting to hear about their day and to learn how much money had been pledged. At the end of the week, more than thirteen thousand dollars had been promised. Alexander added his own name and that of Emma to the list. Each of them donated five hundred dollars.

The Queen also did her part in raising funds for the hospital. With her ladies in waiting, she planned fairs and concerts and theatrical programs. When Emma heard that some important musicians were passing through Honolulu, she asked them to perform for her worthy cause. They were only too happy to help the Queen and hundreds of people turned out on a starry night to enjoy a concert on the palace grounds. Every one who attended contributed one dollar to the Hospital Fund.

When the members of the legislature, who had been dragging their feet over the matter, learned of the King and Queen's success, they were embarrassed because they had done so little. Now they were eager to help.

A downtown building was turned into a temporary hospital while the newly elected trustees, headed by the King, looked for a suitable site. At first, many Hawaiians were

afraid to go to the hospital because they were not familiar with such an institution, but as they heard of the sick people who were cured, they began to go there when they took ill. Soon the temporary facility was filled to overflowing.

Finally a suitable location was found and plans for a new permanent hospital began. Although it took several years to complete, when it was finally finished it was one of the most attractive buildings in all of Honolulu. Everyone agreed that the name of the new hospital should be "Hale Maʻi O Ka Wahine Aliʻi," which means The Queen's Hospital.

Emma was sorry that dear Papa was not there to see it as he had passed away not long after the birth of the Prince. Since it was he who had first inspired her with the dream of building a hospital, Emma knew he would have been very proud that she and Alexander had made the dream come true. Dr. Rooke's friend and colleague, Dr. William Hillebrand, was chosen to run the hospital. It was a difficult task but he worked hard to gain the confidence of the people and minister to their needs. Emma frequented the hospital to assist the doctor as she had helped Papa for so many years.

Because of the efforts of Emma and Alexander, thousands of lives have been saved through the years. The Queen's Hospital is a fitting tribute to the monarchs who so loved their people and did so much to improve their lives.

CHAPTER FOURTEEN

THE PRINCE OF HAWAI'I

After the birth of her son, Queen Emma found it difficult to carry on the demands of court life. A chiefess named Kapi'olani, the widow of Emma's uncle, was chosen to be *kahu-ali'i*, and she eagerly took over the care of little Albert when Emma was called to attend important state functions. Nothing would have made Emma happier than to spend every minute with her son. The life of a queen, Emma knew, was not always what one might wish. She realized that she and Alexander really belonged to the people and soon the baby would be a public figure too. But for now she would love and nurture her child and be with him as often as possible.

Queen Victoria of England was asked to be godmother of the little Prince Albert, and Emma and Alexander were thrilled when the great lady graciously accepted. She promised to send someone to the islands to take her place at the ceremony.

The infant, whom his parents frequently called "Baby," was a happy child with big dark eyes, soft curly hair and a smile that lit up the skies. His parents adored him and he was the pride of the entire nation.

When the little Prince's first birthday approached, a grand celebration was planned and the day was declared a national holiday. In the morning the school children of

Honolulu marched to the palace to pay their respects to the child who would one day rule the Kingdom. Members of the diplomatic corps came to visit, and chiefs, friends and relatives arrived with gifts for the small child who sat alert and bright-eyed throughout the reception. At noon, cannons on Punchbowl and Honolulu Harbor were fired to mark the important occasion.

In the afternoon, a regatta was held at the harbor and thousands of people cheered as long, fast, boats raced across the water. In the evening, long after the exhausted child was fast asleep, the King and Queen entertained at a grand ball in his honor.

The little Prince grew into a handsome boy, full of life, and occasionally a bit mischievous. Because he received so much attention, Emma was careful to see that he was not spoiled. She must have succeeded because, at an early age, people commented on how well he behaved at the official functions to which his parents took him.

When they could spare the time, Emma, Alexander, and little Prince Albert, accompanied by a large entourage, sailed to the island of Hawai'i. They stayed at Hulihe'e Palace, a spacious home on the waters of Kailua Bay, as guests of Princess Ruth, Alexander's half sister. It was a pleasant and relaxing time for the royal family where they could forget the many pressing problems that faced them daily in Honolulu.

The little Prince loved to go fishing with his father. Alexander would paddle his outrigger canoe out into the bay and together they would drop their fishing lines in the water and wait for a fat *kūmū* or *uhu* to bite. The child would proudly present a basket of fish to his mother and when they had been cooked and served, the youngster made sure that everyone at the table knew that he had helped to catch them.

Not long before his fourth birthday, the Honolulu Volunteer Fire Department made the little Prince an honorary member, and part of the crew of Engine Company No. 4. He was delighted to receive a bright red shirt and hat and a shiny silver bugle, exactly like the real firemen. He was even allowed to ride with the firemen on the fire engine in a parade celebrating Alexander's twentieth-eighth birthday. The little Prince gleefully waved at the crowd lined up along the street to watch the festivities, and when they passed the reviewing stand where the King and Queen sat, he stood, and waving his horn and bowing deeply, he shouted, "Look, Papa, we're here!"

Meanwhile, plans for the little Prince's baptism were underway. Word had reached Honolulu that Queen Victoria had sent a silver christening cup that would be used in the ceremony. It was to arrive by ship in the care of

Mr. William Synge, the new British Commissioner to Hawai'i, and Mrs. Synge. He would represent the British Queen in her role as godmother. Victoria had also sent Bishop Thomas Staley to perform the baptismal and christening ceremonies of the royal child.

Emma and Alexander were eagerly awaiting the arrival of the Synges and the Bishop who were traveling on different ships, but days before their arrival the little Prince became ill. His fever rose alarmingly and he clutched his abdomen in pain. His anxious parents immediately called the doctors who rushed to the palace to see what could be ailing the little Prince. After examining him thoroughly, they could not be sure what was causing such severe discomfort. Perhaps it was the heat; perhaps it was something he had eaten. There was no way to know for sure. They could only hope that tomorrow he would feel better.

Emma and Alexander spent a sleepless night beside their young son's bed. The Queen placed a cool cloth on Albert's feverish forehead and clasped his small hand in hers, praying with all her heart and soul for his recovery. Alexander could hardly bear to watch the small body as it tossed and turned throughout the long miserable night. Finally, like arrows from a bow, the first rays of sunlight shot into the room as the tired parents waited to see what the day would bring.

Their hopes were shattered when they saw his condition had worsened.

The ship carrying Mr. and Mrs. Synge and the silver baptismal cup arrived, and being informed of the prince's illness, Mr. Synge rushed to the palace. As the child lay dangerously ill, a simple ceremony took place. The Prince was baptized with Mr. Synge representing both Queen Victoria as his godmother, and her son, the Prince of Wales, as one of the godfathers. The King's brother, Lot, was chosen as the other godfather.

Emma had not eaten or slept for two days so when the ceremony was over, she fell into a restless sleep at the foot of the little Prince's bed. Alexander and the doctors stood helplessly by as his fever soared. Barely an hour passed before Emma was wakened as her son cried out in pain and again she took up her vigil.

The anxious waiting continued. With tears streaming down her cheeks, the distraught mother prayed for a miracle. But it was not to be. On August 23, 1862, the little Prince died, barely three months after his fourth birthday. Emma and Alexander were grief-stricken. The joy and hope that the little Prince had brought to their lives and to the people of Hawai'i was gone. A black cloud covered the sky and the nation wept.

CHAPTER FIFTEEN

THE DEATH OF THE KING

There was a custom in old Hawai'i to give a new name to someone because of a very important event that occurred in his or her life. After the death of Prince Albert, Alexander gave Emma a new name… Kaleleokalani, which means "The Flight of the Heavenly Chief."

Both Emma and Alexander deeply mourned the loss of their beloved child, and it was only their strong faith in God that enabled them to carry on with their lives. They wanted to turn their grief into something positive that would help the Hawaiian people…something for which the little Prince would be remembered.

The King spent many hours at Hānaiakamalama, Queen Emma's summer home in Nu'uanu Valley, mourning the loss of his son and as a way to assuage his grief, he devoted himself to translating the English Book of Common Prayer into the Hawaiian language.

Together, the King and Queen discussed ways in which they might honor the little Prince. They both agreed that there was a need for private boarding schools for Hawaiian children and as a memorial to their beloved child they decided to found two schools, one for boys and one for girls. The English Bishop who had come to baptize the little Prince had stayed on at their request to establish the Church of England in Hawai'i, of which St. Andrew's Cathedral would eventually become a part. He was happy to help Emma and Alexander with plans for the schools. With the help of many other people, they worked hard raising funds and finding suitable locations. Before long, the schools were in operation and it made Emma and Alexander very proud and happy to see the children learning to be good Christians and good citizens of the Kingdom. As a special tribute to their son, at the first anniversary of his death, they selected six Hawaiian children to be educated at the schools at their majesties' expense.

The King donated a large tract of his own land for a church and again, he and Emma helped to raise funds to build a proper house of prayer. A temporary building was used in the meantime and Emma and Alexander attended services regularly.

Since childhood, Alexander had suffered from asthma and often had to take time off from his busy schedule to rest. After the loss of his son, his health worsened and he was often unable to attend to his official duties, which troubled him greatly.

One day, Alexander felt so ill that the doctors were called and the King was put to bed. Although Emma never left his bedside, his illness did not seem to be serious. She was sure that he would recover in just a few days, as he had so often in the past. Much to everyone's shock and horror, two days later the King was dead. He died in Emma's arms, while the doctors looked on helplessly. Alexander was not yet thirty years old. His death followed that of his son by just a little over one year.

Still grieving over the death of the little Prince, the nation was again plunged into mourning. The terrible tragedy was so sudden and unexpected that people could scarcely believe it. By the thousands they tearfully filed through the throne room at the palace to view the body as it lay in state amid an array of black feather *kāhili*.

Outside, thousands of saddened people milled about, many loudly wailing or intoning chants. Some people prayed quietly. As darkness descended over the islands, the crowds refused to leave and the grounds of the palace were aglow with lights from hundreds of torches that blazed throughout the night.

The King's body lay in state at the palace until a proper

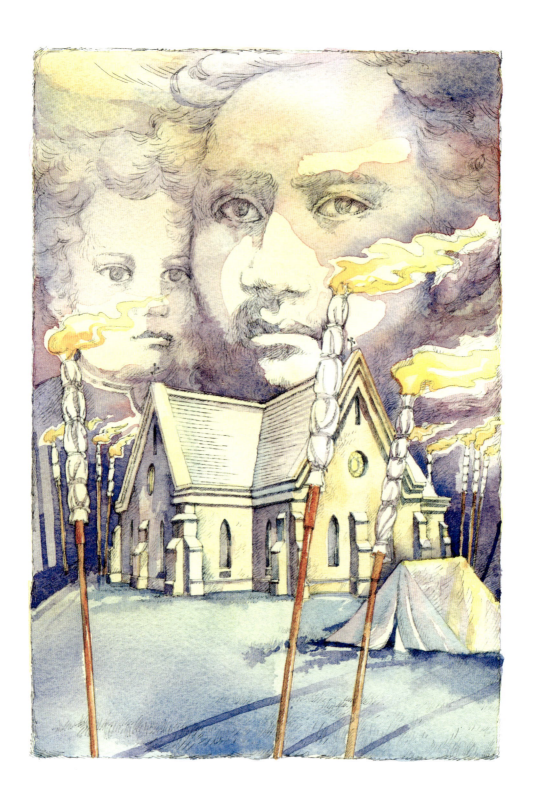

mausoleum could be constructed. Alexander's brother, Lot, who had been declared King as Kamehameha V, arranged for a special plot of land in Nuʻuanu Valley to be the site of the burial place, and work began immediately on a small, cross-shaped chapel. The new King dedicated the land, called Maunaʻala, as a resting place for the royalty of the Hawaiian Kingdom.

When the mausoleum was completed, the funeral took place. Thousands of people were crammed in the temporary Anglican Church that Emma and Alexander had helped to found. Throughout the service, Emma sat close to the casket, her eyes never leaving the face of her beloved husband as his body lay peacefully in the center aisle of the church.

Afterwards a procession formed and the casket containing the late King was transported to its final resting place. The next night, the little Prince was taken to Maunaʻala to lie forever beside his father.

Now, in place of Kaleleokalani, the name which Alexander had bestowed on her at the death of their son, Emma took the name Kaleleonālani, which means "The Flight of the Heavenly Chiefs." The two most important people in Emma's life were gone.

The dowager Queen refused to leave the cemetery,

spending the long and lonely nights in the chilly, damp vault of the chapel beside the caskets of Alexander and little Albert. A small tent was erected just outside the chapel and there Emma spent the days, deep in prayer and overwhelmed with grief, bemoaning the flight of her heavenly chiefs. Those who loved her were worried as it seemed that she had lost the will to live.

When two weeks had passed, Emma left Mauna'ala for the first time since her husband and son had been laid to rest there. Although she would return often, and she would wear the black clothes of widowhood for the rest of her life, Emma decided that it was time to move on. Lady Franklin, who had spent an extended visit in Hawai'i and with whom Emma had become friends, invited her to visit her at her home in London. Emma had long dreamed of visiting Great Britain and the home of Queen Victoria. Perhaps now was the time to make the trip.

CHAPTER SIXTEEN

EMMA VISITS ENGLAND

Emma could hardly wait for the night to end. The long ocean voyage, nearly ten weeks in all, had been pleasant, but now she was eager to arrive at her destination. Emma insisted that her traveling companions, Mr. and Mrs. Hoapili, retire for the night. She enjoyed sitting alone on deck, watching the stars twinkling in the midnight sky and listening to the waves slapping against the sides of the ship. The air was chilly so she brought the heavy woolen blanket up under her chin and snuggled down in the wooden deck chair.

Tomorrow morning the ship would arrive in Southampton. Emma was glad that she had not suffered from seasickness, as many of the passengers had. The sea voyage had agreed with her and for the first time in many months, she was at peace with herself. The deep sadness that had hung over her like a dark cloud was finally lifting.

It was very late when the Queen finally went to her stateroom. She was so tired that she fell asleep as soon as her head touched the pillow, but Emma was back on deck in the early morning's faint light, straining to see the approaching land.

The dock was buzzing with activity as Emma and her entourage made their way down the ship's gangplank and into the waiting carriages that would take them to London. Once settled at Lady Franklin's home, Emma was overwhelmed by the many social events to which she was invited. Everyone she met was entranced with her gentle charm and pleasing personality and was eager to entertain her.

The Queen enjoyed London's foggy weather and marveled at seeing the sights about which she had read since childhood. Although she was familiar with Westminster Abbey from the many books that described it with its high Gothic towers and dozens of pointed arches, Emma was awed by the magnificence of London's most famous cathedral. Nearly all of England's monarchs had been crowned in Westminster Abbey, and some of the country's most famous people were buried there. As she stood in the main hall, Emma realized that it was larger than any room she had ever been in.

Emma spent many days seeing the wonderful sights of London. She was particularly fascinated by Trafalgar Square, the many marble statues, and the enormous Clock Tower that rises above the Houses of Parliament. The most exciting and memorable event of all, however, was Emma's visit with Queen Victoria.

As the appointment had been arranged for early afternoon, Emma spent the morning in nervous anticipation. She worried about whether her clothing would be appropriate and what she would say. After a short carriage ride to Windsor Castle, Emma was ushered into the grand drawing room. The two queens, one from the most powerful country in the entire world, the other from a tiny island kingdom in the middle of the vast Pacific Ocean, met face to face at last. Both widows wore almost identical black dresses, called "widow's weeds." Emma and Victoria smiled at each other and at that instant, the acquaintance that had begun so many years before through letters sent across two oceans blossomed into a special friendship that would last throughout their lives.

The meeting went so well that Queen Victoria invited Emma to return for a second visit to spend the night. Like two old friends, they spent the evening chatting, Victoria eagerly asking questions about Hawai'i and the people who lived there. They spoke of the loss of their husbands and the British monarch sympathized with Emma over the death of her only child.

When Emma left the next day, Queen Victoria gave her a special gift… a bracelet and a lock of her own hair. Emma would always have fond memories of her visit with the

great Queen.

Emma's visit to England was not only for pleasure. The decision to make the long voyage had been influenced by the possibility of raising funds to finally build the cathedral that she and Alexander had so ardently wished for. Emma visited many parishes of the Church of England, and at each one, the people received her with open hearts and were only too glad to contribute to such a worthy cause in faraway Hawai'i.

When winter approached, and the cold weather began to affect Emma's health, she and her party journeyed across the English Channel to spend the cold months in southern France, along the beautiful Mediterranean coast. Her travels continued, taking her throughout Italy, Switzerland and Germany. While in Germany, Emma purchased a baby grand piano which was shipped all the way back to Hawai'i.

Returning to France, Emma visited the beautiful city of Paris where she was regally entertained by Emperor Napoleon III and his wife, Empress Eugenie. On the way home, Emma received an invitation to visit the President of the United States, Andrew Johnson. But first, she would enjoy several days of sightseeing and shopping in New York City.

After more than a year abroad, Queen Emma returned to her home in Hawai'i where hundreds of loyal subjects crowded around the wharf, happy to have their precious Queen safely home at last.

CHAPTER SEVENTEEN

ALAKA'I SWAMP

When Emma learned that she had inherited a large parcel of land called Lāwa'i, on the island of Kaua'i, she was eager to inspect it. From ancient times, the islands were divided into *ahupua'a*, sections of land extending from the mountains to the sea. Dividing the land this way gave the owner access to the fish of the ocean as well as the forests and birds of the mountains. In between, there was usually fertile ground for growing *kalo* and other crops. Emma and a group of friends and servants made plans to visit the area. As it turned out, more than one hundred people sailed to Kaua'i with the Queen.

They found Lāwa'i a beautiful area, abounding with fish ponds, *kalo* fields, and underground springs that provided crystal clear water for all their needs. A rippling stream ran from the mountains to the little bay. Toward the mountains, the land was rocky and barren but Emma soon turned it into a verdant garden. She sent to Honolulu for seeds and plant cuttings and spent long hours in the hot sun, planting, trimming and nurturing the vegetation.

Emma had an adventurous spirit so it was only natural that while on Kaua'i she suggest a journey to a distant place called Alaka'i Swamp. Situated high in the mountains, far from any village, few people ventured to the remote site.

Many people warned her that it was a dangerous trip and tried to dissuade her, but Emma's mind was made up. She set about to find a guide who would lead them up the narrow mountain ridge along a slippery trail, up and down hills and valleys, to the mist-covered swamp described in legends and ancient chants.

Emma found an elderly Hawaiian man named Kaluahi who had made the trip once before and he reluctantly agreed to serve as Emma's guide. The group gathered provisions, loaded them onto their horses, and set out on the journey early one morning. Those who remained behind were fearful that some evil might befall the travelers but Emma was in high spirits and soon everyone was at ease. As they passed through little villages along the way, others joined the group and soon the procession was over a half mile long. Higher and higher they climbed, and as the air turned cooler a fine mist enveloped them.

It was already past noon when they reached the end of the trail. Below them lay a beautiful valley, a patchwork of brilliant greens and yellows sparkling in the sunlight. The trail into the valley was slippery for horses so the riders dismounted and walked them down the winding trail. Suddenly they came to a clearing where the ground was flat and the view below was truly awesome. Emma insisted that they stop to enjoy the scenic vista but their guide was concerned that night would fall before they reached their destination. He tried his best to convince the Queen to keep going but Emma's love of natural beauty surpassed her fear of danger. She sat down on the ground and called for singing and chanting and hula to venerate this wonderful place.

There, on the top of the mountain, high above the sea, a hundred people celebrated the wonders of nature. What a sight it must have been! How strange to hear the strains of ancient chants and songs wafting down on gentle breezes and to see the graceful motions of hands and hips as dancers portrayed the beauty of their surroundings. More than two hours passed before Emma and her group were ready to continue. Much to their nervous guide's relief they reached the bottom of the valley and continued up the other side. On and on they hiked, crossing a wide stream, slipping and sliding along wet, muddy trails, barely visible because of the overhanging branches and vegetation. Finally they came to the swamp itself.

Located nearly at the top of Mt. Wai'ale'ale, the island's highest mountain, the swamp covered an area of nearly ten square miles. Although the word "swamp" conjures up visions of muddy water and unpleasant odors, Alaka'i was truly a beautiful place, shrouded in mist and filled with lush greenery, rare birds and plants. Still, it was frighteningly dangerous. The soggy ground was filled with deep and treacherous holes and anyone who stepped in one might quickly sink to the bottom before he could be rescued.

Emma bravely followed behind the guide, who, conscious of the royal person for whose life he felt responsible, slowly and carefully inspected each stepping place along the way, poking a long staff into the ground to test it for firmness. The six-mile trek across the swamp was slow and laborious. The hikers were careful to follow the guide and not to stray from the route he selected as there was no marked trail. They came to a place where the water covered an area so large that it would have been impossible to continue had not logs of tree ferns been laid down to form an unsteady, floating platform. Everyone, including Emma, was relieved to safely reach the other side.

Twilight was already fading and darkness falling when they entered a thick, gloomy forest. The travelers were wet and cold and very uncomfortable but they had no choice but to spend the night amid the towering trees. Hardly anyone could sleep in the strange surroundings, so Emma entertained them by chanting in her soft clear voice. She even composed a special chant for the occasion.

At daybreak, the group set off for Waimea. The route they took was an easier one and, reunited with their horses, they enjoyed a pleasant and relaxing ride. It had been an exciting adventure that they would all remember.

CHAPTER EIGHTEEN

ALMOST A QUEEN AGAIN

In old Hawai'i, the King's birthday was observed as a national holiday. Stores and schools closed, offices shut down, and parades, regattas, *lū'au*, and grand balls were held to celebrate the special day. Ministers from foreign lands visited the palace to extend their country's greetings and good wishes to the King.

And so it was on this day, December 11th of 1872, the forty-second birthday of Lot, King Kamehameha V. While people came from all over the islands to enjoy the festivities and honor their King, Lot who had been in poor health for some time, suddenly became ill and was ordered to bed by his doctors. His illness worsened so severely that the doctors gave up all hope of his recovery.

Early in the morning, Lot's relatives and those closest to him gathered around his bed, silently praying. Emma's mother Fanny was there, and Emma, who had always been close to Lot, sat beside the bed, although she could barely see him through her tears. His half-sister, Princess Ruth, was present as were many of their former classmates at the Chiefs' Children's School. It was fitting that they should be there since they were the highest chiefs in the land. Her roommate, Elizabeth Pratt, Lydia and her brother, David Kalākaua, Bernice Pauahi and William Lunalilo were among those who gathered close to the bed over which a dark, heavy cloud appeared to hover. Almost the last words that the King uttered were "It's hard to die on my birthday, but God's will be done." It was a tragic climax to his birthday celebration.

Since the days of Kamehameha the Great, whenever the King died there was an heir to succeed him, just as Alexander had ascended the throne of the Kingdom when his uncle, Kamehameha III, passed away. When the little Prince died, Alexander had named his brother Lot as heir to the throne. But Lot had never married and thus had no children, nor had he named anyone to succeed him. Many people believed that in his heart, he wanted Emma to once again be Queen, this time in her own right, but he failed to take the formal steps to name her as his heir.

According to the constitution of the Kingdom, if there was no heir to the throne, the legislature would choose the highest ranking chief for the exalted position. Emma's old friend and classmate, William Lunalilo, a cousin of the Kamehamehas, was elected as King Lunalilo.

Lunalilo, also a bachelor, suffered from ill health and his reign lasted barely more than a year before he too passed away, again leaving the Kingdom without an heir. This time, the choice of his successor was more difficult because not everyone could agree on who the highest *aliʻi* was. David Kalākaua considered himself the most eligible, but many people wanted Emma to be their Queen. The country was torn between the two candidates. The Americans favored Kalākaua because they believed that he would be a better friend to the United States. Because of Emma's close ties to England, the British and many others who admired Emma campaigned vigorously on her behalf. Throughout the land there was great unrest as people argued among themselves who should be the next ruler of Hawaiʻi.

Finally, on the appointed day, the legislature met to cast its votes while more than a thousand people anxiously wandered around outside the courthouse. The wait seemed endless. Finally, over three hours later, the announcement was made: Kalākaua had been elected King!

For a few seconds, Emma's supporters gaped in disbelief. Their disappointment was so great that they began to shout and jeer, and suddenly, they were storming into the courthouse, breaking the furniture and attacking the legislators they believed had been bribed to cast their vote for her opponent. One of the members of the legislature was thrown out of a second story window. It was a dreadful scene, and before the riot was over, many people were injured and valuable government papers were destroyed.

When word of the outcome of the election and the violence that ensued reached Rooke House, Emma and her family and advisors were shocked with the news that not only had Emma been defeated, but that fighting had broken out at the courthouse. It was a sad time for the "Emmaites," as her supporters were called.

When at last the disturbance had been quieted, many of the rioters were arrested and put in jail. The supporters of both Queen Emma and King Kalākaua were bitter; the former, because the Queen had lost the election… the latter, because of the harm that had been caused by the "Emmaites." Emma and the new King were caught in the middle of the tense political situation and both of them did their best to restore peace to the Kingdom.

King Kalākaua paid a visit to Rooke House to offer his regards to the former Queen. Emma later visited the King

at his Palace, seeking the release of the prisoners for whom she felt a responsibility. In time, the bitterness between the two factions receded and the people accepted their new monarch, many of them grudgingly.

Emma had known many bitter disappointments in her life, and this was yet another one that touched her heart. But being the strong and gracious woman that she was, she did not harbor ill feelings toward her former schoolmate, nor he toward her. In fact, the King invited her as an honored guest to the opening of the new legislature over which he would preside, and she accepted with grace. With head held high, she walked with stately dignity down the aisle of the new assembly hall and was seated in a place of honor. On the platform with Emma were Queen Kapiʻolani, the little Prince's former *kahu aliʻi* who had married Kalākaua, and his sister, Lydia, who was now called Princess Liliʻuokalani. They were joined by other members of the new royal family.

Emma continued to play an active part in the politics of the Kingdom and many of her supporters ran for offices in future elections and were often victorious. Her attempt to gain the throne in her own right had not been in vain.

CHAPTER NINETEEN

A NEW LIFE, OLD MEMORIES

Emma was sitting in a *koa* rocking chair on the broad, cool *lānai* of her country estate, Hānaiakamalama. Her dear friends, Lucy Peabody and Elizabeth Pratt, stopped by for tea and Emma enjoyed their company as always. They talked about their old friends and classmates, and life at the Chiefs' Children's School. They laughed as they reminisced about some of the pranks David and James had played on Mr. and Mrs. Cooke. Even David's little sister, Lydia, who was now the heir to the throne and called Princess Liliʻuokalani, had gotten into mischief more than once.

David had recently built a new ʻIolani Palace, much larger and grander than the one in which Emma and Alexander had presided. He had traveled around the world, the first monarch of any nation ever to do so. Yet it seemed only yesterday that they were all children reciting passages from the Bible or racing each other on horseback along the beach at Waikīkī.

What fun it was to relive the old days, Emma thought. Sitting alone now on the *lānai* with its tall white columns, Emma gazed out at the pond with its purple and pink water lilies shaded by the giant paklan tree. Its fragrant blossoms filled the afternoon air with their sweet scent. An occasional gusty breeze sent the small white flowers wafting down to the little island in the pond.

It was quiet now, the only sound the creaking of floorboards as the rockers went back and forth. After a while, Emma dozed off and dreams came quickly. Alexander was sitting in the empty rocking chair beside her and they laughed as little Prince Albert cavorted on the grassy lawn or splashed in the shallow pool under the watchful eye of his *kahu*. "Look Papa! Look Mama!" he called as he somersaulted awkwardly, his curly dark hair tousled by the wind.

Noises from inside the house awakened her and Emma opened her eyes to gaze at the empty chair, the vacant lawn. But still she smiled. In her heart she would always miss her loved ones but Emma had gone on with her life and accomplished many things, as she knew Alexander would have wished. She had never remarried, although there had been many suitors. Her social life had been busy as she had been a very respected member of the courts of Alexander's successors.

She would always remember the grand ball at 'Iolani Palace in honor of the Duke of Edinburgh, Alfred Ernest Albert, one of the sons of her dear friend Queen Victoria. What excitement it brought to the sleepy town of Honolulu when the Duke sailed into Honolulu harbor as captain of the British frigate, Galatea. Everyone wanted to entertain him, including Emma. Emma planned a gala party at her summer home but since it wasn't large enough to accommodate all the guests that must be invited, she built a large room across the back of Hānaiakamalama, which became known as the Edinburgh Room. Unfortunately, the ship could only remain in port for a limited time, and Emma's party never took place. However, she attended all the other events including the grand ball at 'Iolani Palace. Emma was thrilled at the honor bestowed upon her when the Duke gave her his arm and together they led the procession into the dining room for the midnight supper before dancing began. She still treasured the gold and amethyst bracelet he gave her as a parting gift.

Now, with David on the throne, she was invited to all the royal balls, grand *lū'au* and other special functions at the court. As dowager Queen, she remained a highly respected and dearly loved figure in the Kingdom.

What mattered most to Emma, however, were the things she had been able to accomplish for her people. The little hospital, for which she and Alexander had worked so hard, had grown over the years and within its walls thousands of patients had been healed. Hardly a day passed that Emma did not visit the hospital and minister to the sick, laying her hand on a feverish brow and uttering words of hope and encouragement.

Special moments which she cherished deep in her heart were ones that took place not long after her return from England. On March 5, 1867, the cornerstone of the Anglican cathedral was laid. At a ceremony attended by hundreds of people, Kamehameha V had dedicated it "to the pious memory of our royal brother, 'Iolani." The cathedral had originally been named St. Peters, but Lot changed its name in honor of his brother, Alexander, who had died on the feast day of St. Andrew. Although the cathedral was still not completed, its construction was underway and soon the parishioners would be moving from the temporary wooden structure into the majestic Gothic cathedral with its stone arches, tall bell tower and brightly colored stained glass windows. It had been a dream of Emma and Alexander that would soon come true. Emma was also proud of St. Andrew's Priory, the girls' boarding school that grew out of one of the small schools that she and Alexander helped to establish. Administered by Anglican nuns who came from England to teach in the school, it was a source of pride and happiness to Emma. She donated one of her own pianos to the school and took great interest in the progress of the girls who studied there. She frequently invited the students to visit her at Hānaiakamalama, where they enjoyed the country atmosphere and the beautiful surroundings. She often joined them as they picked the enormous, juicy strawberries that grew in Emma's large garden.

The boys' school had also grown and flourished. Renamed 'Iolani in Alexander's honor, the school was situated on a large parcel of land below the Queen's summer palace, and was highly regarded as an excellent learning institution for the young boys of the Kingdom.

Emma often felt Alexander's presence close to her, and that of their dear son. She knew that they were smiling at her, and proud of her for what she had accomplished. In her heart, she knew that the Kingdom and its people, her people, were better off because of the things her love and devotion had accomplished.

Emma died on April 5, 1885. She was not yet fifty years old. Her funeral was one of the largest in all Hawai'i, so loved was she by her people. The procession from the church to the mausoleum in Nu'uanu, where she would lie in peace with Alexander and little Albert, was led by the students of St. Andrew's Priory, dressed in white with black sashes. All of the members of the royal court, including King Kalākaua and Queen Kapi'olani, were there to mourn her passing. As the procession made its way into the valley she had loved so well, raindrops like tears from heaven, began to fall. The people wept and their tears were mixed with tears that fell from the skies, and over it all, a brilliant rainbow arched across the valley.

CHAPTER TWENTY

THE QUEEN'S GIFTS TO HER PEOPLE

The life of Emma Rooke, who became Queen Emma, was filled with great happiness, and also deep sorrow. By the age of twenty seven she had lost her only child and beloved husband. Putting aside her own personal suffering, she turned her misery into good works and positive actions for the welfare of her people. Emma left many wonderful gifts to the people of the Hawaiian Kingdom, and over the years, they have grown immensely, as though she were guiding their progress from the heavens above.

The Queen's Hospital was founded by their majesties, King Kamehameha IV and Queen Emma, who worked tirelessly to raise funds for its construction. The temporary hospital that opened on Fort Street in 1859 had 18 beds and only one doctor. The first permanent building at the present site at Punchbowl Street was equipped with 24 beds. Today, The Queen's Medical Center has 505 acute care beds. On its staff there are 1,200 doctors and more than 3,000 nurses, technicians and other employees. It is the largest private hospital in Hawai'i and a major provider of health care to the entire Pacific basin.

Devout Episcopalians, Alexander and Emma were responsible for establishing that denomination in Hawai'i. Saint Andrew's Cathedral, the seat of the church in the Islands, was a project dear to the hearts of both Alexander

and Emma and they worked hard to raise funds to build it and to bring an Anglican bishop from England to Honolulu to preside over it. The ground on which it stands was a gift to the church from the King himself. Although it was not completed until 1958, long after the death of Queen Emma, Saint Andrew's Cathedral is a tribute to the devotion and dedication of King Kamehameha IV and Queen Emma. Their deeds are memorialized in many places throughout the cathedral.

In 1956, noted artist John Wallis designed a magnificent stained glass window across the west wall of the Cathedral in which the entrance is located. The window tells the story of the life of Christ and chronicles the history of the Anglican Church in Hawai'i. Prominently depicted in the colorful window are King Kamehameha IV, Queen Emma and the little Prince. The Royal Patron's Chapel is dedicated to the memory of the royal family and on display in the Narthex is the baptismal font, a gift from Lady Jane Franklin. It arrived in Honolulu in 1862 and was intended to be used in the christening service for the little Prince.

Saint Andrew's Priory is one of Hawai'i's finest private schools for girls. Emma and Alexander conceived the idea because they believed that it was important for Honolulu to have a school to educate Hawaiian girls. With their majesties' help, a small, wooden school house was built in 1867. King Kamehameha IV personally donated four thousand dollars toward its construction. Over the years, St. Andrew's Priory has evolved into a spacious, modern campus which accommodates 500 students from kindergarten through twelfth grade. Throughout their lives, the King and Queen were strong supporters of the school. One of the royal names given to Alexander was 'Iolani, and this name was given to the school for boys which evolved from the small institution that he and Emma helped to establish. There were 20 students at the Cathedral Grammar School when it opened in 1863. After changes in name and location, the school moved to Nu'uanu and became known as 'Iolani School. When that location was no longer large enough to accommodate the growing student body, 'Iolani moved to its present site along the Ala Wai Canal in 1953. In 1979 'Iolani dropped its all-male admission policy and admitted girls for the first time. In 2003, 1785 students attended the prestigious college preparatory school.

When she passed away in 1885, Queen Emma left a portion of her large estate to The Queen's Hospital. In 1978 some of these lands were transferred to the newly formed Queen Emma Foundation. Now known as the Queen Emma Land Company, the Foundation devotes its funds to the Queen's Medical Center.

During most of her lifetime, there was no library in Honolulu, but in 1884 a small building was erected on the corner of Richards and Hotel Streets, just across from the Palace. The Honolulu Reading Room was established there and Emma soon became an active patron. At her death, she bequeathed to the small library more than 600 books from her private collection. Later, the Honolulu Reading Room became part of the Library of Hawai'i.

In a codicil to her will, Emma bequeathed her vast collection of Hawaiian artifacts including featherwork and wooden bowls to Charles Reed Bishop to be exhibited in the soon to be built Bishop Museum. Emma's collection, and that of her friend and schoolmate, Bernice Pauahi Bishop, comprised the core exhibits of the museum when it first opened in 1889.

Emma had no way of knowing that her country estate, Hānaiakamalama in Nu'uanu Valley, would become a historic house museum furnished with a large assortment of her and her family's personal possessions. Such special objects as the little Prince's red fireman's shirt and silver bugle, the christening cup from Queen Victoria, and his beautiful *koa* cradle are all on display. Queen Emma and King Kamehameha IV's large *koa* bed, along with Emma's piano and rocking chair, are placed much as they were when the royal family lived there. Portraits of the King, Queen and little Prince adorn the walls.

Often visitors to the Summer Palace feel a strange, but kindly presence as they wander from room to room. Perhaps Emma, Alexander and their little son, together once again, are there in spirit, sharing their lovely home with those who come to appreciate the charm and historical significance of Hānaiakamalama.

EMMA'S SCHOOLMATES AT THE CHIEFS' CHILDREN'S SCHOOL

Peter Ka'eo: Emma's cousin. Son of Jane Lahilahi Young Ka'eo and Joshua Ka'eo, descendant of kings of Kaua'i. Jane was the sister of Emma's birth mother, Fanny Kakela Young and her hānai mother, Grace Kama'iku'i Young and John Young II, also known as Keoniana.

Alexander Liholiho: Also known as 'Iolani, was the son of Kīna'u, a daughter of Kamehameha I, and Mataio Kekūanaō'a. Adopted by his uncle, Kamehameha III who named him as his heir. Reigned as Kamehameha IV from 1855 to 1863.

Moses Kekuaiwa: Brother of Alexander Liholiho, Lot Kamehameha, and Victoria Kamāmalu. Died in the measles epidemic of 1848.

Lot Kamehameha: Brother of Alexander Liholiho and Moses Kekuaiwa and Victoria Kamāmalu. Reigned as Kamehameha V after the death of his brother.

Victoria Kamāmalu: Younger sister of Alexander Liholiho, Moses Kekaiwa, and Lot Kamehameha. Died at the age of twenty eight.

James Kaliokalani: Son of Pa'akea and Keohokālole. Older brother of Kalākaua. Died in the measles epidemic of 1848.

David Kalākaua: Son of Pa'akea and Keohokālole. Defeated Queen Emma in the election of 1874 and ruled as King Kalākaua until his death in San Francisco, California in 1891.

Lydia Kamaka'eha: Younger sister of David Kalākaua and James Kaliokalani. Named heir to the throne and ruled as Queen Lili'uokalani until the overthrow of the Hawaiian Kingdom in 1893.

Jane Loeau: Half sister of Abigail Maheha. The mother of both girls was the high chiefess Liliha.

Abigail Maheha: Half sister of Jane Loeau.

William Charles Lunalilo: Cousin of Alexander Liholiho, Lot Kamehameha, and Moses Kekuaiwa. He was the first elected king of Hawai'i. His reign as King Lunalilo lasted just a little more than a year.

Bernice Pauahi: Daughter of high chief Paki and Konia, a granddaughter of Kamehameha I. Married Charles Reed Bishop and was major heir of the Kamehameha lands. Her will established the Kamehameha Schools.

Elizabeth Keka'aniau: Daughter of high chief La'anui and high chiefess 'Owana. She was a descendent of the chiefly house of Keoua. Emma's roommate at the Chiefs' Children's School and her lifelong friend.

Polly Paaaina: Adopted daughter of chief John I'i, assistant to Mr. and Mrs. Cooke.

Information from *The Chiefs' Children's School* by Mary Atherton Richards (Honolulu Star Bulletin 1937) and *Hawaiian Genealogies* Volumes I and II by Edith McKinzie (The Institute for Polynesian Studies 1991.)

GLOSSARY

ahupua'a	Land division usually extending from the uplands to the sea.
akule	Big-eyed or goggle-eyed scad fish.
ali'i	Chief, chiefess, king, queen, royal, noble, kingly.
hānai	Foster child, adopted child. To adopt a child.
hula	A Hawaiian dance; to perform a Hawaiian dance.
imu	Underground oven. Food cooked in an imu.
kāhili	Feather standard, symbolic of royalty.
kahu	Honored attendant, guardian, nurse.
kahu ali'i	Royal guardian in the family of high chief.
kalo	Taro. A kind of aroid cultivated since ancient times for food. Kalo has been the staple from earliest times to the present.
kamani	A large tree at home on shores of the Indian and Pacific oceans.
kapa.	Tapa. A cloth made from the bark of *wauke* (paper mulberry) or *māmaki* (a small native tree.)
ki	Ti. A woody plant in the lily family.
kihei pili	Two sheets, as of kapa, printed percale or patchwork, sewn together at edges, used as bed covering.
koa	The largest of native forest trees, *Acacia koa*.
kou	A tree found on shores from East Africa to Polynesia.
kūmū	Goatfish.
lānai	Porch, veranda.
lauhala	Pandanus leaf, used in weaving.
lu'au	Hawaiian feast, named for the *kalo* tops always served at one.
moi	Thread fish.
mu'umu'u	A loose gown.
oli	Chant that was not danced to.
paklan	Also call ylang ylang or lanalana. Noted for its heavy scented flowers.
pāpio	An important game fish.
pikake	The Arabian jasmine, a shrub with dark green leaves and small, white, fragrant flowers used for lei.
poi	The Hawaiian staff of life. Made from cooked *kalo* corms, pounded and thinned with water.
uhu	Parrot fish.

Glossary based on: *In Gardens of Hawai'i* by Marie C. Neal (Bishop Museum Press 1965) and *Hawaiian Dictionary*, by Mary Kawena Pukui and Samuel H. Elbert (University Press of Hawai'i 1981.)